# Sammy's Quest

### Written and Illustrated

### by

### Nina Ashton

*For my Grandchildren*

*Thalia, Abigail, Gabrielle & Liam*

Copyright © 2020 by Nina Ashton

All rights reserved. No part of this publication may be reproduced, distributed, or transmitted in any form or by any means, including photocopying, recording, or other electronic or mechanical methods without the prior written permission of the publisher, except in the case of brief quotations embodied in critical reviews and certain other noncommercial uses permitted by copyright law.

ISBN 978-0-5787721-9-6

First published in 2020 by Doodle Arts Books
https://doodlearts.com

*Doodle Arts*

Printed in the USA

The Admiral went back to his green bush and soon his mate flew over to join him. He was happy to see her at last.

Then he thought about how sad he would be without her, and he felt bad for Sammy.

Suddenly, a Swallowtail butterfly fluttered near his bush.

The Admiral charged at the Swallowtail to chase him away from his perfect spot.

"Whoa! Easy, Sir," said the Swallowtail. "I'm Sammy and I'm looking for my mate Sally. She told me to meet her on the bush in Gramma's garden."

"Well, she's not here," said the Admiral. "This bush is for my mate only. Now go or you'll scare her away."

"OK," said Sammy, and he fluttered away down the river.

But soon, Sammy fluttered by again. "Sally wasn't down there. Is she here?"

Again the Admiral charged at Sammy. "No, she's not. This bush is for my mate, not for your mate. Get out of here."

"OK, OK," said Sammy, and he fluttered away up the river.

The Admiral went back to his post on the willow hoping he'd seen the last of Sammy.

But Sammy came right back again. "Sally wasn't up there either. Is she here now?"

"NO, NO, NO!!!

For the last time:

She's not HERE!

Now go away and don't come back!"

"Oh no," cried Sammy. "She must be lost." Sammy swooped sadly away from the river, afraid that he would never find her. He had been to every bush in the area - but no Sally. Where could she be?

He raced back across the river and into the spooky thicket.

"Good luck!" cheered the damselfly.

Sammy flew past the gazebo and over the gate.

"Steady on," purred the bobcat.

He flew into the forest.

"Where?" asked the owl, waving.

"Still looking!" Sammy called back.

At last he found the tidy garden - and there she was!

She had been waiting all this time on a pink bougainvillea bush.

"I'm so happy you're here!" said Sally. "Were you lost?"

"I guess so," said Sammy, laughing.

For the rest of the day Sally and Sammy sipped nectar together on their pink bush.

And the Admiral and his mate sipped nectar together by their green bush.

In doing so, they all made Gramma's garden even more beautiful.

# Would you like to color Sammy?

# Fun Facts about Butterflies

## Role in the Ecosystem

**Food Supply** — As pollinators, they help maintain our food supply. When they flit around sipping nectar, they carry pollen from one flower to another. This leads to the production of fruits and seeds that create more plants. The fruit, seeds and plants are our food and food for many other animals. Butterflies and caterpillars are a food source for birds and other animals.

**Pest Control** — Some caterpillars feed on garden pests like aphids.

**Pollution Control** — Some butterflies even reduce pollution by absorbing carbon dioxide.

## Western Tiger Swallowtail Butterfly

It is named for its striking coloration and the tails on its hindwings, which look like the feathers of a swallow. Rarely resting, they are very active and the males really do actively patrol for females. Swallowtails are the largest butterflies in North America.

## Lorquin's Admiral Butterfly

The males really do like to bask in the sun on a tip of a bush and wait for females to come along. They are fiercely territorial, even attacking large birds. The females like to lay their eggs on the underside of willow leaves, so that their hungry caterpillars have a nice juicy breakfast when they hatch. From time to time these butterflies will sip from bird droppings and dung. Eeeeyuuu.

What else might be going on in Gramma's Garden?

Tales from Gramma's Garden is a book series designed to inspire in children a sense of wonder and appreciation for wildlife and the intertwining ecosystems in our world, starting with our own backyard and neighborhood.

Printed in the USA
CPSIA information can be obtained
at www.ICGtesting.com
LVHW071022091123
763115LV00063B/999